I Was an Orphan

An Autobiography

Alton Watkins

ISBN pb: 9781527278721
ISBN ebook: 9781527278714

Cover design by: Mark Made Group Ltd.

DEDICATION

I would like to dedicate this story to my dear wife, Yvonne, who cannot walk anymore because she has multiple sclerosis.

TABLE OF CONTENTS

INTRODUCTION

Some fifty years ago, I remember studying a poem, 'The Ice Cart' by Wilfrid Gibson. The first few lines went thus:

Perched on my city office stool,

I watched with envy while a cool

And lucky carter handled ice...

And I was wandering in a trice,

Far from the grey and grimy heat

Of that intolerable street,

O'er sapphire berg and emerald floe,

Beneath the still, cold ruby glow

Of everlasting Polar night.....

Just as that distraught office worker's thoughts and imagination were sent soaring to cooler, idyllic climes on that hot, intolerable day, triggered by the lucky carter handling ice, so too did my thoughts soar to the distant past. But unlike the office worker, mine were about when, living in Trinidad, I was well and truly trapped in the poverty cycle and my journey to break out of it.

What actually triggered my thoughts was a lecture, which I was fortunate enough to attend, given by the then Archbishop of Canterbury, the Most Reverend Dr Rowan Williams. It was on the occasion when my *alma mater*, Canterbury Christ Church University, celebrated its 50th birthday. I was sitting in the audience, a very proud man, knowing that it was this university that gave me the start to higher education and beyond. In fact, just sitting there was one of the high points of my life.

The exact moment came when Dr. Rowan Williams in his lecture posed the questions, 'What is the purpose of a university, and in particular, what is the purpose of an Anglican university?' When I heard those questions, I became very excited because I knew that, by using myself as an example, I could answer them both.

What then were the thoughts that were stirred and what does the notion 'trapped in the poverty cycle' really mean?

THE BEGINNING

The women in our family were always strong, hard-working, brave, adventurous, decisive, and full of confidence and common sense. They were uneducated, but they were not stupid or foolish. Except for my mother's common-law husband, I cannot remember any man playing a dominant, significant role in our lives. My maternal grandmother, Martha, left the island of Antigua with her husband and three young daughters seeking a better life. By the time she got to Trinidad, sometime between 1910 and 1920, her husband was already dead. She arrived with three young children, all girls, Celestine, the youngest, Agnes, my mother, the second, and Violet, the eldest.

For a single woman to set off across the seas with three young girls to a strange land takes some doing. Some may describe it as foolhardy. I can well imagine how difficult it was for this one-parent family. All three girls got pregnant fairly early in their lives; Violet, the eldest, migrated to New York in 1925, leaving her firstborn, a boy named Luther, behind. She got married there and had two more sons, Willard and Harold. She passed away in 1957 and Willard in 2013.

I do not know where my grandmother first settled when she arrived in Trinidad, but my very first recollection of her was living in a barrack yard, 44 Lewis Street, Woodbrook, Port of Spain. There was a well-to-do family fronting the barrack yard and they were No. 44. But so were we. The barrack yard was the lowest form of accommodation, and our grandmother was living there with the youngest of her three children, Celestine, along with Celestine's daughter, Winifred.

At this time, my mother, Agnes, was living with her common-law husband, my sister, and me in the seaport town of San Fernando, in the south of the island. It was a very blissful existence. We lived in and owned our own home. There was ample room for us to play with neighbour's children and relatives. My sister and I each had our own room. There was a big yard with lots of exotic fruits: guavas, mangoes, sapodillas, kymet, sugar apple, soursops, oranges, golden apples, downs, and coconuts. We had pets to look after, and there were always chickens, ducks and even goats running around in the yard. My special pet was a mangy dog called Plus. I loved that dog, but despite all my affection, I ended up with a sore head covered in mange!

Schooling started for us at Mrs Brown's kindergarten in Broadway, San Fernando. One day a boy about five years older than me came and stayed. He soon became friends with all the older boys in Broadway. His name was Cyril. It was always exciting times watching these bigger boys at play. There was a kite season, and Cyril and his friends made their own. These kites were works of art, and one in particular, the Mad Bull, would seemingly sing as it madly flew high up in the skies, skilfully controlled by its owner.

The top season soon followed. Cyril and his friends also made their own tops. The wood chosen was always from the guava tree because of its hardness. These tops had to be durable, because after some kind of a top-spinning game, the loser could have his top chopped up by the winner. When the marble-pitching season came in, all the boys, young and old, got their marbles out. I remember having beautiful coloured marbles, but not for pitching. For me, they were just beautiful things to have so I used to horde them.

Another favourite pastime of the older boys and men was the catching of songbirds. I always fancied a pair of parakeets (not singing-birds), but I was never lucky enough to have them given to me.

A treat I always looked forward to was the annual excursion, by train, organised by the local Anglican church to one of the many picturesque savannah areas relatively far away from San Fernando. The train journeys were particularly delightful; the hustle and bustle at each of the village stations as we stopped to drop passengers off and take on water, the smell of the smoke-like steam, the hiss of the puffing engine, and its shrill whistling, but above all, the hordes of vendors who always bore down on the stationary train with their trays of confectioneries; sugar cakes, in vivid red or white, tooloom, tamarind balls, kurma, never-done, pone, caramel, nut-rock, currant rolls, salted and unsalted peanuts, chana; all Trinidadian delicacies, as far as we children were concerned. Our home was a few yards from Charlie's, the well-known purveyor of souse and black pudding, and this delicacy was often part of our menu.

Ours was truly a comfortable lifestyle and a very happy family unit. But this was not to last. Suddenly, abruptly, all of this came to an end. I was about five and my sister four. (I always find it odd that my sister cannot remember anything of these early years). My mother's common-law husband died and, for reasons which I still cannot understand, we had to leave our home in a hurry. Our social status changed overnight, and we became a one-parent family with all that that entails. The good times came to an end. Our standard of living went from well-to-do to zero, and we found ourselves members of the underclass. What made the situation more complex was that my mother was pregnant.

That was when we moved to Port of Spain to live with our grandmother, Martha, which was my first encounter with the barrack yard. To say it was a culture shock would be an understatement! It was also at this time that it gradually dawned on me that Cyril was in fact my brother, my mother's eldest child. He was living with Martha, our grandmother, and, from time to time, came down to San Fernando to stay with us.

THE SECOND PHASE
OF MY LIFE

James Cummings, in his excellent book *Barrack-Yard Dwellers*, describes the barrack rooms as being 'like the boxes horses are shipped in. A long line of ten by twelve feet boxes nailed together, with a window and a door allotted to each.' Six people living in one room in a barrack yard is no fun. We, the children, slept on the floor. We never had much to eat. Granny and Celestine were domestic servants; Celestine worked for the well-to-do family fronting the barrack yard and Granny elsewhere in the town. The leftovers from their employers' dinner tables were brought home from work late at nights and that was all we got, if we were lucky. Schooling was very sporadic, and for the 12 months we were there, we never had any friends of any kind. No pets, nothing.

Winifred, Celestine's daughter, did bring some cheer to our lives. She took us for early morning walks that were refreshing and enjoyable, especially along the coast. She also introduced us to Sunday school at the local parish church, St Crispin's. I remember being given a beautiful biblical stamp on each visit to insert in a special booklet. I always looked forward to receiving those stamps. The problem, though, was that occasionally we attended other churches.

Our mother, who had remained in San Fernando, working as a domestic servant, eventually came and took us to be with her once again. From then on, for the next two years, it was moving from one barrack room to another; first in Port of Spain then back to San Fernando. Our mother had given birth to a son, Arthur, but I just cannot remember who was looking after him. On the odd occasions when she was with us for a few days, we were very happy as a family. On these occasions, she would take in a few shirts to iron for clients. I was the one who would take them back to their owners, collect the few shillings, and come back home. Our mother always spent that money on us. Then she was off again, working as a domestic away from home.

It was at this stage of my life that things could have gone badly wrong for me. With our mother away working most of the time, we were on our own, invariably without much to eat. I soon attached myself to groups of boys who went marauding through the countryside, catching crabs in the mangroves, and risking death by drowning as we followed older boys swimming at Flat Rock, a well-known spot on the nearby coast. Staying out late at nights was becoming prevalent, and sometimes I would find myself lurking in the local shops, waiting for the chance to steal anything edible.

Despite our mother being away so frequently, when she did come home, she quickly sensed that I was fast becoming a delinquent. She had to act swiftly. And she did. She knew that Granny had put the child Luther, whom Violet had left behind on her way to New York, into an orphanage run by the Church Army, an arm of the Anglican Church. My mother decided that that home was the place for my sister, Arthur, now about two years old, and me. Once she had made her mind up, proceedings went by rapidly; the necessary papers were acquired through the courts and we soon found ourselves in the home's hospital, where all new arrivals had to spend a few days in some kind of quarantine. This was in the year 1937, two years before the Second World War broke out.

And so started one of the most significant phases of my young life. It was perhaps the most meaningful act that our mother did for us, and I will always be thankful to her for doing so. My formative years were greatly shaped by the seven years I spent there. And so the second phase of my young life began. I was seven years old.

LIFE IN THE
ANGLICAN HOME

When Dr Rowan Williams, in his lecture, posed the second of his questions, 'What in particular, is the aim of an Anglican university?' I became very excited again because, rhetorical question or not, I believed I knew the answer. In fact, as a product of an orphanage ran by the Church Army, an arm of the Anglican Church, I felt certain I knew the answer.

I am not going to compare Tacarigua Orphanage with a university — I would be very foolish to do so; however, it was an educational establishment, broadly speaking, and most importantly it was an establishment run by the Church Army. I had never heard of the Church Army before, and even after spending over half a century in England I still know nothing about them! Most people always think I am talking about the Salvation Army!

The purpose of an Anglican university and an orphanage or residential school, providing that the latter is run by the Church Army, are precisely the same: to hold or to convert all its students or inmates to Anglicanism. What is very different is the methods or style they use to achieve their aims and, of course, the curriculum they follow.

The former will use humane methods with the concepts of freedom, understanding, respect, rationality, and religious understanding as the cornerstones of any educational activity. The latter will use rote learning and indoctrination, with religious studies a major component of the curriculum supported by a very rigid form of discipline. The church building would never be far away from major activities. However, the methods they used at Tacarigua Orphanage did me no harm; what is important is that later on in life I was able to understand what those methods were, and why they were used, and I was able to use them to my advantage.

THE TACARIGUA ORPHANAGE

Tacarigua Orphanage was founded in 1847 when Trinidad was still a British colony. It is sited on 25 acres of land nestling at the foot of the Northern Range in the Valley of the Tacarigua River. The St Mary's Anglican Church, built in the Gothic style, was sited opposite the home, separated by a road, the Eastern Main Road.

Tacarigua Orphanage was a semi-self-contained unit. On the western side, running parallel with the river, was to be found the babies' and girls' dormitories along with the two-storied school building, the kitchens and other ancillary buildings. The inmates were organised under some kind of number system. The girls were known as No. 2s. The babies had their own specialist quarters. My brother, Arthur, was not old enough to be with me so he was put in the babies' sector. Each grouping had their own space in the immediate vicinity of their dormitories to conduct their daily lives.

On the east side were the bigger boys, the No. 1s, with their dormitories, the trade shops, the captain's and matron's living quarters, offices, etc. There was even a dynamo for providing the home's electricity which was always breaking down. The younger boys, the No. 3s, with their dormitories, were to the north. Occupying the central position was a large, paved recreational area reserved for official gatherings of all inmates, and other similar functions.

To the north of all this was a much larger grassed recreational area for football, cricket, and other school sports. There were a number of plots scattered around, where the bigger boys, under supervision, cultivated such crops as corn on the cob, sweet potatoes, and pigeon peas. This activity was mainly a training and educational enterprise. (After I left the home, an arable farm was established there). Many of us also had our own very small piece of ground where we grew things as a hobby: flowers or vegetables. Our main source of food was the wholesalers in Port of Spain. Every month, supplies were brought to the home by horse-drawn cart all the way from Port of Spain, eight miles away. Rice and root vegetables were the staples with ample supplies of fresh fruits.

The St Mary's Church was the village parish church, so the inmates from the home congregated with the locals during services. The school in the home was like any other village school, and the teachers, all Anglicans, came from towns and villages from the outside. The headmaster was one Mr Stanley, a firm disciplinarian, but a fair one. One of his sons, Carl, attended the school (I remember him as not particular bright) and one of his daughters had a key post in the orphanage; she ran the office, and knew the history of every child that entered the home.

The curriculum of the school was interesting. Subjects such as singing, reciting, writing, spelling, reading, drawing, geography, arithmetic, history, hygiene, drill, and gardening were taught. Yes, there was a library, a rather small cabinet with about a dozen books!! The school had its own garden, a neat, tidy, well-organised plot of land, where the growing of crops was practised. These included root crops, maize, tomatoes, cabbages, peas, and greens. There was even a miniature mango tree.

The headmaster, Mr Stanley, took a great deal

of pride in his school garden. I believe at one time there was friction between the matron and headmaster. The matron thought that she had the right, with basket in hand, to march into the school garden and help herself to the choicest of vegetables and greens! It soon stopped, but how Mr Stanley managed to do so, I never knew. I always enjoyed leaving lessons and going to an Indian community across the river to get manure as fertiliser for the growing crops. Mr Murray, one of our teachers, was always the one to accompany us on these very relaxed, enjoyable trips.

The home also had a brass band that provided many of the local orchestras with trained musicians. The teaching of music had nothing to do with the school. The teachers of the band came from the National Military Band based at the St James Barracks in Port of Spain. In fact, many of the musicians of the National Band were recruits from Tacarigua Orphanage. The band used to do their practising in an open courtyard near to the bigger boys' dormitory. I used to spend hours listening to some wonderful tunes, and I soon got to know the names of some of the best operas, overtures, symphonies and symphonic poems ever written and their composers.

Listening to those wonderful musical compositions at that time was a purely emotional experience; understanding came later on. My only regret about the home is that I never took the great opportunity I had of learning to play a musical instrument. Famous names in the music world of Trinidad who were ex-inmates from Tacarigua Orphanage include Sel Duncan, George Scott, Watty Watkins, Gerry Jemmot, Lincoln Grant, Michael Smith, better known as Whitey, and his brother Blackie, Robbie Robinson, Thomas Elder, Kenneth Lane, Holis Alexander Newman and others.

An off-shoot of the band was the communication system that was used when all inmates had to perform a function at the same time. With 500 of us roaming far and wide on the vast grounds of the home, a special communication system had to be adopted. The answer was the bugle. The bugle can be heard over long distances. It is highly effective in communicating simple information and orders to a large number of people. A series of bugle calls were therefore used: one for wake up, one for assemble, one for dismissal, one for meal-times, one for fall in, one for re-call and, finally, one for lights out.

All inmates reacted to these very distinctive commands with alacrity. There was one in particular for all of us who were fond of breaking bounds. Whether you were up in the hills of the Northern

Range, or scrounging food at some Hindu wedding, or swimming in the river, on hearing the piercing sound of the re-call command of the bugle, everything was dropped, and a mad rush made back to the home for roll call. Woe to anyone who got there late!

There was another orphanage, run by the Roman Catholics in Belmont, Port of Spain, and they also provided leaders and members for all the various musical bands on the island and abroad. Superintendent Prospect, a former inmate from Belmont Orphanage, became leader and conductor of the National Band. Previously, all the superintendents were English or Irish men. Dr Eric Williams, the first black man to govern the country, soon put a stop to that. Bandsman Prospect was sent away to England for further musical studies. On his return, he was made superintendent of the National Band.

When Superintendent Prospect retired, bandsman George Scott, from Tacarigua Orphanage, took over. George Scott's history is very remarkable. It was said that his mother was an inmate and his father one of the officers in the home. Suffice to say, he was put in the babies' specialist quarters. He grew up in the orphanage, passed through all the age groupings, became a junior officer, and from there got into the National Band as a clarinet player. He then rose to become the leader of the National Band. He, too, is now retired and still alive.

Most boys and girls had the opportunity to learn a trade as technical/vocational training was on offer: shoe-making, carpentry, tailoring, joinery, masonry and plumbing for boys; embroidery, beauty culture and dress-making for girls. I had a shot at tailoring, and on my very first attempt at stitching something, stitched one of my fingers onto the cloth! Needless to say, that was the last time that I was seen in that workshop.

Under the leadership of an excellent teacher, one Mr Fitz-James Williams, our school won an island-wide reciting competition twice; Lancelot Lougheid and Lloyd Webb were the two participants. Under the leadership of the headmaster, Mr Stanley, we won a Bible-class competition on several occasions.

Other well-loved teachers were Mr Woodruffe and Miss Griffith, who was very gentle and had an excellent rapport with the infants and juniors. She played the piano and taught the whole school to sing. She got married to Mr Woodruff, and they went off to live in Barbados, taking an inmate by the name of Punchin with them. There was the Thomas family who had a long and illustrious career at the home as teachers, administrators, board members and genuine friends of the inmates. One of them even got married to a former inmate. I can distinctly remember a group of us being taken to the nearby town of Tunapuna to see a film, *Jessie James,* and sitting next to me was one of the younger Thomas brothers. It was my very first film and I was curious and excited. However, he reassuringly explained to me what was happening, when necessary.

Sports and athletics were part of the scene, and our school always took part in outside competitions. I remember taking part in many sporting events but I was never good enough to make the school teams. In athletics the only event I ever won was a sack race, and this is ironic, as you will see later. Many of us used to break bounds, go roaming in the wooded mountains to the north of us looking for mangoes and other fruits, or go swimming in the nearby river. I always wondered why the further one went up the river the bigger, the rounder the boulders became. It was at Christ Church that I got the answer.

There were two special events that we, the children, always looked forward to. One was an annual event that took place a few days before Xmas. Dignitaries of the churches, leading commercial businesses, government and the community at large were invited to see all inmates performing various skills. This event was known as 'Toy Day'. Formation marching to the tunes of the brass band, sculpture formation with climbing bodies, and other events were performed. Then the toys were distributed! The proceedings were brought to an end when hundreds of tennis balls were thrown at us from the windows of a nearby dormitory. The mad scramble to retrieve as many balls as possible was great fun. The other event that we looked forward to was an Easter treat given by Miss Audrey Jeffers, a well-known national figure on the island, but this was rather a low-key affair.

However, the biggest treat for me was when our mother came to visit us. We were always overjoyed to see her. On these occasions she would shower us with jars of jams, cakes, sweets, toothpaste, soaps, brilliantine and coconut oil. Lucille would receive dolls, and Arthur and I wonderful clock-spring cars and trucks. There were always tears in my eyes when she had to leave us. I remember my mother presenting me with a marvellous fire engine. You wound the spring up, and off it went with all bells loudly ringing. The first night it slept with me under my cot, and someone tried to steal it in the dead of night. On lifting it off the ground, the sudden loud ringing of its bells woke everybody up in the vicinity. The thief was caught red-handed, and he, shame-faced, ran back to his cot.

The home also had a cadet corps, with a sergeant from the local Voluntary Military Force training us as young soldiers. What was odd, and somewhat comical, was to see us parading to the sound of the accompanying brass band, guns on our shoulders but with no shoes on our feet. You should have seen the astonished smiles on onlookers faces!

It must be remembered that I am writing about the era when the Church Army ran the place. It was the era of Captain Williams and his wife, Mrs Williams, the matron. This was between the years 1937 and 1945. Resident female staff caring for the girls and younger boys were known as nurses, and residential male staff were addressed as Mister, Sir, or Captain. One of the senior officers, Mr Gaskin, and his wife Nurse Laddy, a trained medical nurse who was in charge of the Home's hospital, I remembered as very caring and kind (not all inmates would agree with me). I did household chores for them, and I was always rewarded with some kind of pocket money. They were truly *in loco parentis*, as they were with all the others. The domestic chores that I did for them have served me well throughout my life.

All inmates had to be christened, baptised and confirmed if their parents had not already done so. I was already christened but had to be confirmed. These are all necessary conditions of being an Anglican. Confirmation classes were held in the parish church across the road. I remember them as being very pleasant. Every Sunday, the bigger boys and girls had to attend church and the younger ones attended Sunday school. We had to know all the religious festivals, not only Xmas and Easter but the minor ones as well. The season of Lent I will never forget; for us a time of solemn austerity, with plenty of hymn-singing; who can forget the hymn, 'Forty Days and Forty Nights', almost frightening for us children. And what about Good Friday with the three-hour long service! However, come Easter Sunday, and the lusty singing of those joyful alleluia Easter hymns was something to take part in or to be listened to. Every church festival had its specialist hymns, sung to some wonderful, wonderful, melodious tunes, and we knew most of them. The Church Army did a good job on us, and I became an Anglican for life.

Children behave, react, and adapt differently in certain environments. It is the nature/nurture argument rearing its head. It could well be the case that many ex-inmates would have a view of the place contrary to my own. That is understandable, but I have no regrets. To quote one of its mottos, 'For children who were developmentally and educationally challenged, the home aimed at restoring their confidence, developing their self-esteem and becoming competent in a number of crafts and vocations in civil society.' I left Tacarigua Orphanage when I was 15 in 1945. I could now write, spell, read, and do sums. The education I received there was basic, elementary, but it was good for what it was, and it was a start.

My sister, Arthur and I returned to live with our mother, now living in the village of Boissiere in Maraval, sited in terrain that was long and relatively narrow with a river flowing through. The main road ran parallel with the river, with mountains on both sides. (Walking up the main road on my first visit from England to Boissiere in 1979, I instantly recognised the area as a very good example of a river valley). On getting to Boissiere, we had a very pleasant surprise; we discovered we had an addition to the family, a younger brother by the name of Toney.

Meanwhile, Granny had managed to secure a loan from Miss Audrey Jeffers, a well-known public figure, the same lady who spearheaded the Easter treats to us orphans in the Tacarigua Home. The house was built on the barrack yard principle; two

12 x 12 rooms joined together, but constructed with proper building materials. Celestine, the youngest of Granny's three girls, was living next door with her daughter, Winifred.

Granny, now ailing, lived in one of the rooms, and my mother, Lucille, my sister, Toney, Arthur and I lived in the other. There was ample room to move about in the yard but obviously not in the room. There was a mango tree right on the border of one of the adjoining properties and an avocado (zab-o-car) tree on the border of the other adjoining property. Both fruits are delicacies in Trinidad, and we were delighted that they were there. On the surface, our social status changed for the better. But our mother was still working as a live-in domestic.

By now my mother had become a happy-clappy worshipper, and nothing is wrong with that. It was something meaningful to her, and it was the method she chose to keep in touch with God. It kept her busy and happy. However, the Church Army people had done such a thorough job on me that I found myself looking askance at other religious groups. For the first time, my mother and I did not see eye to eye. I stopped attending all those happy-clappy religious gatherings with her, sometimes held in residential homes or small churches. I began to attend an Anglican Church, St

Crispins, in Woodbrook, Port of Spain. Winifred, Celestine's daughter, had introduced us to this church when we had moved in with them in Woodbrook.

I was now 16, and about to move into another phase of my life that was very exciting indeed, and, I am pleased to say, with my mother's blessing and helping hand.

VILLAGE LIFE IN BOISSIERE

L ife in Boissiere was perhaps different from the average village life in Trinidad. This was because Boissiere was a suburb of Port of Spain, the capital, very much the largest city on the island. There was an excellent transport system, with buses every 30 minutes and plenty of taxis to get you to the centre of town in good time. (Those were the days before maxi-taxis came on the scene). Many of the villagers had bicycles to get to work in the city without any difficulty. It was only about five miles away.

I was very happy living in Boissiere; I made many friends there. All my spare time was spent on its recreation ground playing cricket and football; it was on this same recreation ground that I discovered that I could run long distances faster than any of my peers, propelling me to become a leading athlete on the island. I remember a certain young man, Tom from Tobago, joined us on the recreation ground claiming that he could outrun me in any flat race. We decided that 10 circuits of our recreation ground was a mile. Tom and I started together. When I completed the race, Tom still had 5 laps to go!

Slash and burn farming was practised on both sides of the mountainous valley that was Boissiere. The dense vegetation was set on fire and burnt down. Root crops, such as cassava, sweet potatoes, and yams were planted in the ashes along with pigeon peas, tomatoes, and pumpkins. When all the fertility of the soil was used up, the farmer would move to another area and repeat the whole process again. It was a type of subsistence farming, but some of the farmers did have markets to supply. I knew a few of those farming families, and I and their teenaged children would go up to the mountains, not to assist in the farming activities, but to gather fruits that grew wild in abundance up there, especially mangoes. It was something to do, and it kept us out of mischief.

It was because I was living in Boissiere that

I met the two persons that were instrumental in getting me a successful five-year apprenticeship at the Trinidad Guardian, the largest publishing company in the West Indies, and it was by living in Boissiere that I met my first wife, Barbara.

Sadly, it was around that time that Granny died. A year or so later Toney died. He and a school friend were climbing a lucky-seed tree in someone's garden. It was believed that if you kept one of these seeds on your person, harm would not come your way. He fell from the tree on to a concrete fence with the rubble, ironically, crushing his head.

Finally, it was from Boissiere that I left for England in 1956. All these occurrences were life-changing ones. And yet, paradoxically, it was whilst living in Boissiere that I felt more trapped in the poverty cycle than ever before. How could this be? First, despite my mother's optimism, we were still a one-parent family. She was still working away from home as a domestic servant, and Lucille and I had to fend for ourselves. Also, it was at this stage of our lives that Lucille and I drifted apart; if there was cooperation between us things could have been much better. She made it very clear that although she was my sister, we were not close; we were never friends, and we saw the world through different eyes. Arthur was now making himself a nuisance by stealing anything that he thought could be useful to him. Cyril had moved into Granny's room when she died, and he helped us occasionally. He was now running a confectionary business.

However, my mother soon got me a part-time job with one of her employers, a Mrs Pashley, doing odd jobs for her. I also managed to get an evening job serving drinks and washing glasses in one of the leading entertainment venues, the Country Club, at that time reserved for those of European descent only. The money from both was not much, but it was helpful.

Then came the big break for me, again through my mother. She was now worshipping in some kind of a Baptist Church, run by an American vicar, whose name I have long since forgotten. How my mother knew about apprenticeships I never knew but, suffice to say, she got this vicar to put in a word for me at the Trinidad Publishing Company, and so did Miss Pashley, my mother's employer. I got my five-year apprenticeship. Despite all our hardships, my mother was always looking out for me. I think it was much more than the inherent bond between mother and son! She knew that I was not satisfied with my life and that I wanted to move on.

THE TRINIDAD
PUBLISHING COMPANY

I n 1945, the Trinidad Publishing Company was based on St Vincent Street, Port of Spain, and was organised into two sections. The commercial department published books, magazines, and labels, while what was called the production department brought out three newspapers: a daily newspaper, called *The Trinidad Guardian*, an evening newspaper, called *The Evening News*, and a Sunday newspaper called *The Sunday Guardian*. In every sense, it was a modern newspaper business.

When one says one is a printer, one could be doing one of many jobs. When I turned up on a Monday morning to start my apprenticeship, I was put into the commercial department to be trained as a compositor. The first task for any compositor is to set type, by hand, and to do that you are put in front of a large tray of lead letters. Each letter, *a, b, c,* and so on are to be found in their own small cell-like compartment in a fixed, orderly arrangement so as to facilitate the compositor when he has to choose the appropriate letter for each word to build up his sentence, then his paragraph and, ultimately, the completed page. I hated it.

I was then transferred to the production department, where I was assigned to what we called the stereotype department under a Mr Dato. This was the department that dealt in hot, molten lead, casting flat plates from matrices mainly for overseas advertisements and comic strips. I stayed there for perhaps two years. I was then transferred for the third time, and it was what I wanted; at last, I found my niche, Ludlow operating. I loved it.

The Ludlow was a machine used for setting the headlines for newspaper articles and for designing and producing advertisements. For instance, a sub-editor will write his heading for a particular story and send it down to the Ludlow operator to be set up in type. On many occasions, the Ludlow operator may have to change a word because of length, or to change the size of the type that the sub-editor originally asked for.

With an advertisement, the plan of it on paper would be sent to the Ludlow operator with the size and type-face to be used and the layout. More often than not, the Ludlow operator would choose different specifications from that of the original plan. For me, it was a very creative enterprise, and, ironically, my elementary education was no problem at all. I had two very skilled tradesmen, a Mr Roy Collins and a Mr Verett who taught me everything I needed to know about Ludlow operating.

I greatly enjoyed my ten years at *The Trinidad Guardian*. They were a very important part of my formative years. There were many skilled tradesmen there you looked up to as role models: Austin Cambridge, Roy Piper, Andy Hernandez, Olonzo Brown, Oliver Knights, Sunny Paris, Roy Waterman and many others. Another colleague I must mention was George John, who is sadly no longer with us. He kept me very busy on the Ludlow. As a sub-editor, he always came down to find out about things like the size of type for his headings. He was always careful about such things. It came as no surprise to me that he went on to become the leading journalist and newspaperman of the day in the West Indies. We met up again in England when he became the editor of *The Jamaican Gleaner* (England edition). We became firm friends until his death in Trinidad a few years ago.

Coinciding with the good years at *The Trinidad Guardian,* other wonderful things were happening to me. My athletics career blossomed and, in 1954, I won every road race promoted in Trinidad and a few on the track. One of the biggest athletics meeting held in the West Indies was the Southern Games, held at Point-a-Pierre, Trinidad, promoted by one of the oil companies. I won the 10,000 metres there. Another big athletic meeting, ran by another oil company at Point Fortin, invited me as a special guest to take part in their 10,000 metres race. I won that too.

Not only was I a member of *The Trinidad Guardian* Sports Club, but I became a member of Hawks Sporting Club, a club run by the Hoddet family in St James for their middle-class ex-college friends. I also joined a Woodbrook club by the name of Humming Birds, based at the Youth Centre, a sporting facility run by the Church Army. *The Trinidad Guardian* held a few athletics meetings during my time there, and I won the 1-mile race on all occasions.

A few enterprising businessmen got together

and organised an athletics meeting in Boissiere on the recreation ground, Tapia. I duly won the mile race and the 10-mile road race that opened the meeting. The trophy for that 10-mile road race was donated by a Boissiere businessman and landowner, Mr William Scott, and I am pleased to say that it is still in my possession, as are all the other trophies. They are proudly displayed in a cabinet in our sitting room in Purfleet, England, and are of enormous sentimental value to me.

I became a member of the Adventurous Club formed by Freddie Kissoon. Other members were David Huggins, an apprentice at *The Trinidad Guardian*, Peter O'Neal, who, I believe, was still at school, and a few others whose names I cannot remember. Our most memorable adventures were our ascent up Trinidad's highest mountain peak, Mt. Aripo at 2,936 ft above sea level, and then El Tucuche, the second-highest. The footpaths leading to the peak of Mt. Aripo were densely overgrown with tropical vegetation, and we literally had to, using cutlasses, hack our way through to the peak. The Americans had originally got to Mt. Aripo before anyone else and had laid a small concrete plaque exactly on the highest point. When we reached the top, we hurriedly gathered around the plaque, for night was fast closing in, took a few photographs, and hastily started our hazardous descent back to the lowlands. Incidentally, Freddie Kissoon went on to become one of the most celebrated playwrights in the West Indies, while Peter O'Neal found success as one of Trinidad's leading actors.

In 1948, the first Olympic Games after the Second World War was held in London. I was a teenager then, but I was winning all the local road races and a few on the track. Trinidad held trials for selection. I won the 10,000 metres race, but they only sent sprinters and weight lifters. There was no room for me. Of course, I had no chance of winning any event in the Olympics, but I could have gone for the experience! My friends used to call me the *Black Zatopek.*

Every Corpus Christi day, the sister island of Trinidad, Tobago, held an athletics meeting organised by the Scarborough Club. In 1954, Trinidad sent a representative side managed by a Mr Alexander, a former cyclist, and I duly won the 3-mile flat there. The trophy presented by the Hon. A.F.T. James is still in my possession!

Those days were good, and I remember them with fondness. But I was acutely aware of my shortcomings. You remove the facade of seeming happiness, of what appeared to be normality, contentment, and what was revealed? Lack of a proper education, never really having enough money and enough food to eat, moving around with colleagues far above my social calling (my shortcomings acutely showing up even more), living in sub-standard housing, and, despite my mother's common sense and constant striving to do the right thing, part of a dysfunctional family.

Many a morning I never had money to take the bus to work so I walked. Many a morning I never had a proper breakfast, and I am not talking about bacon and eggs, baked beans, tomatoes, mushrooms and toast, followed by a mug of genuine English tea; my breakfast tea could have been a leaf plucked from some bush or tree growing in our yard and boiled, with a little condensed or evaporated milk added for a cuppa. Bread could have been what we called fry bakes, roast bakes, or local bread from the bakery. During my apprenticeship days, I never had the privilege of any such sumptuous fare. It cost nothing, so it was always a cup of bush tea. And for most of the day, if I did not have the penny to buy a rock cake and a glass of mauby, that was it.

Of course, there were days when I had proper

meals and had the bus fare for getting to work. But those days were the exception to the rule! My wage as an apprentice was very small, and most of it went back to money lenders! After work, I would walk the five miles back to our village recreation ground to join my friends in a game of cricket. After the game, back home, a cup of bush tea, and that was the day done. How I am still alive, how I became a top athlete by West Indian standards, to use a well-known Trinidadian phrase, *God only knows!*

The Oxford English Dictionary gives the meaning of the word *'proud'* a *'feeling pride or satisfaction in your achievements, having an excessively high opinion of yourself, and having self-respect'*. I certainly was a proud man, and I went about my daily chores with my head held high. For instance, my mother, so good-natured, always had the notion that some of the people she worked so hard for were her genuine friends. One such family, the Lings, from Woodford Street, New Town, had a birthday party for one of the children. Our mother dressed up me and my sister and sent us off to this party. On arrival, we were quickly dispatched to the servants' quarters, and the doors firmly closed behind us. I was so ashamed that we found ourselves in such a dehumanising situation that, after about 10 minutes, I dragged Lucille out of that room, and we walked the four miles back to Boissiere.

I am of the opinion that few people knew my true social and economic position. I want to make it abundantly clear that it was not because Trinidad was a Third World country — it was not; it was because we were so desperately poor! In 2007, my wife and I visited Trinidad. We met a Frenchman at the guest house where we were staying. We became firm friends and he wanted to know my story, so I told him. He listened very intently and at the end he said, 'Alton, I am amazed that you do not appear to be angry!' What was there to be angry about? As I saw it, my destiny was in my own hands. In any case, being angry would have destroyed me.

Things changed somewhat for the better when I completed my apprenticeship and became a fully-qualified tradesman, a Ludlow operator. Shortly after, in 1955, I got married to a girl from the village of Petit Valley, a genuine, old historic village (and again, sited in a typical river valley) with most of the inhabitants at that time descendants of the French/Spanish/African workers from the old cocoa and sugar cane plantations. Most of them spoke a fluent French-Spanish patois.

I settled down fairly well to married life. I

made many friends there. One of them, Andrew Lara, a very good long-distance runner and former rival. I am pleased to say he is still alive. But there were drawbacks; serious rum-drinking was one of their main hobbies. I soon joined them in this activity, but I played it cleverly. I always had far more coke in my glass than rum. I believe that is why my liver is still in good condition.

Meanwhile, my sister Lucille had got a job in a local shoemaker's shop. It also came to light that when our mother's common-law husband died, the property was left to Lucille. When she became of age, she sold it. In 1956, with the proceeds from the sale of the house, she came to England, where she trained at the Prince Edward VIII Hospital in Windsor and qualified as a nurse. She got married sometime after that, then she and her family migrated to New York, USA where she still resides.

Despite my marriage, and despite experiencing a much better quality of life than before, I still was not satisfied with my life. So, in 1956, at the age of 28, I followed my sister and set sail for England, temporarily leaving my wife behind. This really was the best thing that ever happened to me. *The Evening News* sports reporter of the day wrote thus:

'The latest of Trinidad's athletics 'exports' leaves for England today by the S.S. Lucania in the person of Alton Watkins, 1954 long-distance champion. As an athlete Watkins leaves a long list of achievements behind obtained in a comparatively short time. As a sportsman the frail bespectacled marathon man will be remembered for his modesty.'

MY FIRST SEVEN YEARS IN ENGLAND

The voyage to England was most eventful. My mother and a few friends were there to see me off. It was in September 1956. Sadly, it was the last time that I saw my mother. I do not know how many were on board the ship, but there were a few hundred. We did not have cabins as such, but areas where various groups lived, if you like, and slept. I believed there were cabins for those who knew about such things and could afford them. The food was adequate, with plenty of cheap dry wine. There were the usual stowaways, but they were never discovered.

Our first port of call was the Canary Islands,

in those days a rather barren, dry region, but I cannot remember too much about them. Our next port of call was Barcelona, Spain. It was in that city that we saw television for the first time and were introduced to Bacardi and Coke. It was also there that I had my first glimpse of a European cathedral, but it was closed.

The next port of call was Genoa in Italy. We visited a few rather pleasant night clubs whilst there and were surprised at how many of the young clubbers spoke English. It was in Genoa that we took the boat train, travelling through France to Calais, where we boarded the ferry across the English Channel to Dover, England. At Dover we took British Rail to Victoria Station, London. There were the usual hordes of West Indians that are always there to see and greet new arrivals, and one acquaintance from my Tacarigua days was there. His name was Ralph Fields. I have never seen him since, and I often wondered what became of him.

There used to be a cliché-like phrase commonly heard expressed in England, even in the newspapers of the day, that West Indian immigrants literally believed that the streets in England were paved with gold. For me, they *were* paved with gold, metaphorically speaking! In London, for instance, where I settled, there were hundreds of further

45

educational establishments, staffed by highly-trained specialist teachers; there were at least half a dozen of the world's best art galleries; some of the best museums of the world were to be found in London. London had its cathedrals, some of them over a thousand years old, virtually on the spot where organised religion and government first started. Rivers always do something to me! There was the River Thames, at that time home to one of the leading, busiest ports of the world. And, of course, the Festival Hall.

As a printer by trade, there were hundreds of printing firms, where, despite the closed shop principle, relatively lucrative employment could be had in non-union firms. The residential streets in themselves were lined with similar-looking houses, block after block, and that was not by accident. In central London, all around St Paul's, there were still huge craters in the ground, bombed-out sites, inhabited by stray cats.

For me, the problem was how to make sense of this new amazing world. How to interpret it! I was determined that I had to get into the mainstream of English life. I would not be satisfied with staying on the periphery, leading a life as though I was still in Trinidad. The answer, therefore, was education, education, education; so, two weeks after arriving in London, I enrolled at the North Western Polytechnic in Kentish Town to do my GCE in English and English Literature at evening classes. I had managed to rent a room from a Trinidadian acquaintance who was living in Highgate. I had arrived in England in September 1956, and the Xmas of that year I got a temporary job as a platform porter at Mt. Pleasant post office sorting out bags of letters. Come the end of Xmas, came the end of the job.

Ever since I could remember, I always had to read my daily newspaper. I continued to do so in England. From among many, I chose *The News Chronicle*, not because it was a good newspaper, but because it published all the printing vacancies in London. I duly saw an advertisement for a Ludlow operator in a non-union firm, in Hither Green, south-east London. The printing industry was highly unionised and highly paid. Without a union card, though, you could not get a job. However, there were many small printing firms not affiliated to the union. These were invariably run by Jews who did not want to pay the high wages of the unionised firms. The printing unions, by maintaining a closed shop, ensured there would be an artificial scarcity of labour, hence maintaining high wages for their members and, to a certain extent, security of tenure. In essence, that was what the closed shop was all about.

I knew that I could not get a Ludlow operator job in a union firm, so I took a three-month course, full-time, at the Monotype School in Fetter Lane, Fleet Street. On completion, and because of my general experience in the printing industry, I was admitted into the Monotype Casters and Typefounders' Society. I was now working for a decent wage inside the industry, rather than being exploited from the outside. It was at this juncture that I was able to send for my wife who I had temporarily left in Trinidad. We did not spend much time together. She soon got into a hospital in Hastings to be trained as an assistant nurse. She did very well for herself, because she went on to further studies, passed all her exams, and became a fully-registered, qualified nurse. By this time, though, all the goodness in our marriage had disappeared, and so we divorced. She is still living in London, and still working, and is comfortably well off.

CELESTINE AND FAMILY

I want to digress for a short while, as it was about this time that Winifred, now grown up with five teenage children, along with her husband, migrated to England from Trinidad in 1960, bringing with them her mother Celestine, the youngest of the three original sisters. Winnie's children, Wilfred and Dexter, the boys, and Brenda, Judy and Beverley, the girls, went on to complete their few terms of comprehensive education. They all got jobs and merged into the mainstream of urban life in London. They are all now married and have children, and in Wilfred's case grandchildren. They are happy, confident and are at ease with themselves.

Wilfred spent almost the whole of his time

in England working with and for the Notting Hill Carnival. He still finds the time to be a promoter of Black musicians, both from Jamaica and the USA., organising concerts for them not only in England but also on the continent. From the very beginning of life in England, Celestine was always very happy. Other than Yvonne, she was the only one to send me a birthday card each year. Winnie's family is a very close-knit one, large and mostly young.

Celestine, a relatively young woman when she arrived in England, found herself growing old gracefully in a warm, caring, loving environment. She went on to reach the age of 99 and just missed out on receiving the Queen's customary best wishes to those reaching a century. She passed away in 2005. Wilfred, for his tireless work among the Black West Indians, popularising their music and culture, in England and Europe, was awarded the OBE by Her Majesty the Queen.

Because of my new job, I moved from Highgate, north London, to Hither Green, south-east London. I necessarily had to move from the Kentish Town Polytechnic to the Catford School of Commerce. I did very well there, and when I applied to Canterbury Christ Church College it was with GCE passes in English, English Literature, economics, economic history, British constitution, mathematics and sociology.

What I always found interesting was that there were always a few Trinidadians in all the evening classes I attended. Because they were all ex-college boys or former high school pupils, they always tended to see themselves as superior to anyone with only an elementary education, or worse still, from one of the orphanages in Trinidad. They saw themselves as an elite class. Modesty was foreign to them. What was so good about evening classes was that the lecturer always started from first principles. What mattered most was not what kind of school one attended in the past, but one's IQ and how motivated one was. As a result, many of those ex-high school pupils were found wanting.

COLLEGE LIFE IN THE CITY OF CANTERBURY

When I applied, in 1964, to do teacher training at Canterbury College of Education, I was very much a mature student. I had a choice to do the 2-year training course for mature students, but I chose to do the 3-year course that was available to all other students. Firstly, because I did not want anyone to say 'he only did the 2-year course for mature students', and secondly, I wanted to gain the maximum experience of a university education. I started university life in September 1964. The place was still being built. I was installed in Thorn Hall, a male residential hostel on the campus. It was a happy place; I was not a brilliant student, but I worked very hard. Whereas GCEs were relatively easy, relying on memory to a large extent, at university level one had to get inside the subject as it were, with analysis of whatever was being taught, and interpretation required to achieve a deeper understanding and find the truth.

I did two main subjects: geography and combined studies. Combined studies was a mixture of subjects, to give one a broader picture of the world. The underlying thought behind it was that students would find areas of particular interest which they could pursue later on in life. We also did curriculum subjects, which were all the subjects that were taught in schools in England. I became very interested in art, architecture, and maths. But more of that later. Information technology was in its infancy, and I remember attending a few lectures at the new, emerging Kent University, up on the hill, where we saw one of the first computers. It was as big as a London double-decker!

On the whole, I enjoyed university life at Canterbury. I made many genuine friends there; the cross-fertilization of ideas and the sports (cricket, football, squash, and hockey were all played) were the important by-products as it were. I was not good enough to make any of the college teams, though. My athletic days were now behind me. Whilst at Canterbury I briefly met a Trinidadian student, also doing teacher training at the nearby Nonington College. We graduated the same year. She was the daughter of a well-known Trinidadian/Guianese footballer, 'Golden Boy' Rodrigues. I often wonder if she went on to become the Minister of Education for Trinidad and Tobago!

MY TEACHING CAREER

I left college in June 1967, but only with a teacher's certificate, and immediately started to look for a teaching post. It was not easy, and it was not until January 1968 that I found one. I saw an advertisement in *The Times Educational Supplement* for a teacher of geography, and I wasted no time in applying. The school was Ockendon Courts, in South Ockendon, south Essex. Suffice to say I got the post, teaching geography and English. It was a secondary modern, mixed, and a forward-looking one because it had a sixth form, with pupils studying subjects at GCE level. The great majority of the pupils, however, were studying their subjects at CSE level, an exam that was seen as inferior to the GCE. The teachers were all very hard-working and dedicated.

I taught my specialist subject, geography, throughout the school, except the sixth form, and some English at CSE level. I was a strict disciplinarian, and the pupils recognised me as such. Mr Larwood, the headmaster, was well-loved and respected by all the pupils, parents, and staff. He was very kind and understanding towards me and guided me through my probationary year. I had to tone down my discipline rather quickly, a matter of adapting, while still being recognised as a teacher that was not to be messed with. It was a source of great joy when I received official confirmation that I had satisfied the authorities of my teaching ability, by doing well in my probationary year:

'Dear Mr Watkins, I am pleased to inform you that as you have completed to the Department's satisfaction a scheduled course of training, you are eligible for the status of qualified teacher. I have been asked by the Secretary of State to convey his congratulations and to wish you many years of happiness in the teaching profession.'

I was now a fully-fledged school teacher. My mother in Trinidad was the first to hear the good news. It was around this time that I bought my first car, a Ford Escort, and I have had a car ever since. These days, however, we only use our car, a Ford KA, for local shopping, etc.

FURTHER EDUCATION

Around the time I left Canterbury, the teaching profession was re-organised, making it a university discipline with a degree course. It was a chance missed. I therefore enrolled at Avery Hill College, Eltham, to do the In-service Teacher Education Course, with geography as my main subject. Other subsidiary subjects were taught as well: sociology, psychology, philosophy, amongst others. Because it was a degree course, the teaching was far more rigorous and of greater depth than at Canterbury.

I got a great deal of satisfaction in writing up my dissertation. It did not take you right to the frontier of knowledge, but it was a major undertaking.

It was about farming in the Borough of Thurrock, and it is one of my prized possessions. There had to be an outside adjudicator for its final assessment, and to my pleasant surprise it was my former geography lecturer from Canterbury, a Mr Winter.

Avery Hill was not an Anglican University, but run by the local authority. The lecturers were of various faiths and came from various backgrounds. Because it was a part-time course, there was not that intimacy and camaraderie amongst the students that was to be found at Canterbury Christ Church University, or Tacarigua Orphanage for that matter. Nevertheless, I enjoyed my stay there, and I cannot remember ever missing a lesson. I got my first degree and went on to do an extra year, to get the Degree of Bachelor of Education (Honours). It took me about six years to complete the course, during which time I was still teaching full-time at Ockendon Secondary Modern.

THE REORGANISATION OF
SECONDARY EDUCATION
IN THURROCK

In 1971, Thurrock reorganised its education system on comprehensive lines. Overnight, all the secondary schools became comprehensive schools and, for whatever reason, teachers had to re-apply for their jobs at their schools, or at any other school in the borough. I applied for a post as a first-year tutor at Torells Comprehensive and got it. I was to teach geography throughout the school and some English, as well as carrying out my duties as a year tutor. A year tutor is a pastoral post. Torells Comprehensive was organised with an upper and lower school, and my post as year tutor was with the first and second-year pupils in the lower school.

My duties included visiting the feeder junior schools in our catchment area to speak to the incoming pupils and answer their questions to allay any fears of coming to a much bigger school. I had to collect all their records giving information about their age, IQs, reading age, disabilities, parents, behavioural problems, illness, etc. Using all the information from their records, they had to be put into mixed ability forms, boys and girls. Usually, it was an eight form entry. A Mr Ron Wallace, an experienced teacher of many years standing, was head of lower school and was of enormous help to me and a true friend. It was he who allocated the teachers to their forms. From then on, I had to work very closely with the lower school form teachers.

I took turns with another year tutor, a Mr Hasket, to conduct morning assemblies. School report evenings had to be organised, parents had to be contacted for all kind of reasons, sick notes and holiday forms all had to be looked at, sporting activities had to be organised amongst the pupils, museum visits, annual one-day trips to Calais in France, parents' evenings, open days; all these activities one had to take in one's stride. It must be mentioned here that in a large comprehensive school, such as Torells, the cooperation of all staff was essential, and I am pleased to say I never had cause to complain. Comprehensive education was a new concept, and all the schools were still feeling their way.

WHAT IS A COMPREHENSIVE SCHOOL AND WHAT DO WE MEAN WHEN WE SPEAK OF COMPREHENSIVE EDUCATION?

From secondary modern to comprehensive education was a gigantic step. The truth is education in England is never static. Revolutionary changes are taking place all the time. So, what do we mean when talking about comprehensive education? Any country or place, Trinidad or Timbuktu or wherever, can build a school and define it as a comprehensive. However, in England, comprehensive education comes with a philosophy, a rationale. This philosophy, this rationale, has to be understood before comprehensive education can make sense.

In fairly recent times, the social set up in England was still based on the class system. There was the working class, the middle class, the upper-middle class and the so-called blue-blood families. The education system reflected this class system. There was one type of school for the working class, the secondary modern, one type of school for the middle classes, the grammar school, and still another for the upper classes, the private/public schools.

One country yet three different social classes, each with their own distinctive form of education. Not only that, over 70% of the population were working class, and yet their education in the secondary modern schools was only rudimentary! Lots of potential talent was left untapped! What made the situation more urgent was that the industrial advantage that the country held over others was now slipping away. Do not forget that the Industrial Revolution began in this country! So, what is a comprehensive school?

Definition

It is a school taking practically all the children in from a district, irrespective of class, colour, or creed, apart from those with special educational needs and those attending independent schools, and educating them under one roof.

The Curriculum

At Torells, comprehensive, the subjects offered were English, French, mathematics, history, geography, art, physical education, music, science, woodwork, domestic science, and religious studies. Most of these subjects were taught in mixed-ability groups. Although, I knew one head of department who always used his powers to get all the pupils with high IQs and good behaviour into his class! The rest went to other members of his staff!

Teaching Methods

At Torells, team teaching was the preferred method of teaching. I remember geography, history, English and RE combining to be called humanities. A key lesson would be given in the main hall to a full year group, followed by the children going back to their individual classrooms with their teachers. The key lesson just heard would be discussed and analysed, followed by written work from problem questions set by the teacher. Many kinds of visual aids were used. Information technology was not in vogue then. There were some teachers who disliked team teaching, but they had to carry on and soon they got into the swing of things.

At Torells, I worked under three headmasters and one headmistress. What I can say now is that within the boundary of the school, they were very powerful individuals. But they all had certain virtues in common: they were wise, sincere, hard-working, and tended to know the weaknesses and strengths of all their staff and most of the pupils.

At this time, I was acting head of geography, as the previous head had died some time ago. In due course, a new head, Paul Redrop, was appointed. If there ever was a born teacher, then he was one. He was excellent! He had physical presence. He had the ability to bring any subject alive; he knew his subject inside out, his approach was both authoritative and yet down-to-earth. He always had the attention of all his pupils. In so far as classroom activities were concerned, he was excellent in all. He was well-liked by the pupils, and apparently got on well with members of staff. And yet, we two never were friends.

However, I consider myself a good teacher, and I always felt that I could work with the best of them. I also knew that I was a highly-qualified teacher and a hard-working one. I was always the first to arrive in the morning, and I worked at Torells for many, many years before going off ill. That is unheard of in comprehensive schools in England! So, despite the frosty atmosphere between me and Paul Redrup, I was still able to teach ably and efficiently. I enjoyed my duties as a year tutor enormously, and that frostiness between me and Paul was only a minor irritant.

On the 27th March 1992, a school inspector came to observe me teaching a year 9 class. A copy of his report was given to me, and this is what it said:

'Mr Watkins clearly has very good control over the class. They were quiet and attentive as he delivered a clear and well-illustrated talk on Tyneside. Questions were raised and answered in the talk and the reasons why Tyneside became so important industrially should have been made clear to all.

After 20 minutes Mr Watkins turned the board to reveal an essay title and points to be covered and the task was set. Again, the pupils worked quietly and efficiently and there seemed little doubt what was required of them. After a further 10 to 15 minutes 4 pupils were asked to read their introductory paragraphs. All were clear and different from each other. It was evident that the talk had been understood and the pupils were able to discuss the topic in their own words.

The last hour on a Friday afternoon is not an easy time to sustain children's attention and effort. It is a measure of Mr Watkins' work over the years that this was achieved and the objective of the lesson was fulfilled.'

Whilst all of this was going on, I got married to my second wife, Yvonne. Yvonne, originally from Guiana, South America, passed through the education system in England from primary to the secondary stage, going on to the sixth form. On leaving school, she went into the Civil Service as a trainee typist. From this humble beginning, she went on to work in many government departments in Whitehall before reaching the Department for Transport as a personal secretary to many of the heads there. All together, she worked in the Civil Service for 42 years.

On nearing retirement, in July 2001, she and I, as her husband, were invited to one of Her Majesty's Garden Parties. Further honours came her way, for when she finally retired in 2007, she was awarded by Her Majesty, the Queen, the Imperial Service Medal *'in recognition of the meritorious services which you have rendered'.*

Yvonne, unlike me, had no notions of getting into the mainstream of English life. She was already in it. She is not only my wife, but a very good friend. We go and do everything together. All the years I worked at Torells, I always addressed all members of staff as Mr or Miss; to me, it was the natural thing to do. To illustrate our different upbringing though, I remember Yvonne saying to me, 'Alton, why do you always call members of staff Mr, Mrs, or Miss so-and-so? Why so formal?' I just could not give her an answer.

It was, of course, a throwback to my Tacarigua Orphanage days where, with the Church Army people, one had to behave in the appropriate manner always. Not that I am complaining. Yvonne, on the other hand, went through a liberal educational system in England as a child. She was always in a more relaxed, friendly atmosphere, so it was natural to address all her peers by their first names, as is the custom here.

It was also at this time that I got the news that my mother had died. She had diabetes and had been ailing for the past year or so. However, she lived long enough to enjoy the successes of her two children living abroad. Lucille had already broken down the two-room, barrack-like home that was ours. She replaced it with a two-story modern house. Our mother lived in it quite happily before she died. I could not attend the funeral for various reasons, but I telegraphed some money to Lucille, who had flown down from New York to oversee the funeral.

For many months after my mother's death, I

always felt guilty that I could not attend her funeral; what made it even worse was that I had a letter in my pocket with a £10 note that I never got round to posting. My guilty feeling remained until a strange phenomenon occurred, which took me back to one of my favourite hymns: 'God Moves in a Mysterious Way' by William Cowper. The fourth verse goes like this:

Judge not the Lord by feeble sense,

But trust him for his Grace;

Behind a frowning providence,

He hides a smiling face.

A few days after my mother's burial, I had a strange dream. I thought that I had been woken up by a touch on my shoulder. Turning around, I saw my mother with a radiant, happy, smiling face looking at me but gracefully gliding away. I kept running after her, whispering 'Tanty! Tanty! Tanty!', but she drew further and further away and finally disappeared. I knew then that my fears were unfounded, that she understood why I could not attend her funeral. Whenever I think of my mother now, there is always a smile of happiness, of contentment, on my face, sometimes with a tear or two, even after all these years. I will never, never forget my mother!

Changes were taking place in our catchment area, thus forcing changes at Torells. Because of falling birth rates and de-population, our school roll declined sharply. The school found itself over-staffed. During this time, many teachers were glad to be offered early retirement packages. The humanities had to get rid of one of its teachers, and the headmaster, Mr Brasher, offered it to me.

At first, I was reluctant to take it, but after giving it some serious thought, I went back to the head and told him I accepted. He told me it would not make me rich, but that it was a good package I was to receive. It was made up of my annual pension, my lump sum, my redundancy payment, and an enhancement that the headmaster saw as adequate. I have since learnt that a senior member of staff went behind my back to grab it! Needless to say, we paid off our mortgage and the rest of the money we invested.

At the end of the summer term 1992, and after 45 years in education (including my student days), 21 of those at Torells, my full-time career working at any one school came to an end.

What gave me the most satisfaction is the education I received that got me there. That education completely transformed the course of my life. I also take pleasure in the fact that I was able to assist so many pupils to reach their full potential. On the way, I met many good human beings from among pupils, parents and staff. My contacts in the printing industry enabled me to secure apprenticeships for two former pupils from the Ockendon Secondary School. That alone was justification for the extra increments on pay that I got as a mature student when I started teaching. Even the rogues I met in both schools were likeable ones.

There was quite a lot of socialising among staff at Torells; parties at some members' homes, end of term drinks at the local pub, and the occasional trip to the live theatre in London. And, of course, there were the numerous educational trips to London that the pupils were taken on. They were all enjoyable affairs. These were always well received by both pupils and staff.

I remember one in particular, a trip to Covent Garden with 5th formers, to see *Madame Butterfly*. Accompanying teachers were John Laith, Dave Edwards and me. Half-way through the production, I had to go to the toilet for a pee. I believe I fainted, for when Mr Laight found me, I was flat on my back still holding my penis in my hand! A sit down in the fresh air and all was well again.

Of course, I made mistakes along the way; we all do. What is important is that I learnt from those mistakes. As in Trinidad, in poverty, I walked with my head held high, so too at the end of what I consider a very successful teaching career, I walked away with my head held high.

I went on to teach part-time for a number of years in all manner of schools and finally retired from that, permanently, in 2003. I then discovered that retirement for Yvonne and me still had a lot of good things in store for us.

LIFE AFTER RETIREMENT

One of the places I visited very often as a new arrival in London was the National Gallery in Charing Cross. I would walk from room to room viewing the art without understanding anything. I knew that it should be an experience of revelation of some sort but, try as I did, nothing was ever revealed to me. I used to leave the place very frustrated. That is, until I met a student at Canterbury Christ Church. I was in the second year, she in the first. She came from India and was Anglo-Indian, of mixed parentage. One Sunday, breaking a few college rules, I took her down to London. And guess where I took her, to the National Gallery in

Charing Cross.

It was an experience I will never forget. The first room we entered was one filled with historical and religious paintings. Each painting we came to, Sadia (a fictional name) knew what it was all about and explained it to me. I was very much surprised. I followed that young lady from room to room, taking in everything she said about each painting.

I do not know if she knew what technique, style, or pigment the artist used, or if she knew anything about linear or aerial perspective, or foreshortening, or anything about the illusion of light or space in the paintings, nevertheless, it was a start. The risk I took by breaking a few college rules was well worth it. A few weeks later, a group of students from Holland visited our college. Sadia fell in love with one of them, got married, and off she went to live in Holland. I often wonder how she fared.

I also had a similar experience with cathedrals. I always knew that the architecture of cathedrals, and buildings in general, was something very interesting, and, of course, to know about the contents and history of cathedrals could be very exciting. Whilst studying at Avery Hill College, I met a friend who was mad about cathedrals. It so happened that we went on a camping holiday to Normandy, France by car. Amongst others, we visited Mont-Saint-Michel, a wonderful experience for me. This ancient Romanesque monastery, perched up on the hill surrounded by water at high tide and treacherous mud and quicksands when the tide recedes, had many secret treasures. You gain entry by going across on a causeway. We got in and were able to visit many of its ancient and historic rooms: including the refectory, cloisters and vaulted halls. When we left there, I had a feeling of fulfilment.

Our next stop was Rouen Cathedral, which had been made more famous by the Monet paintings. We entered and looked around and Myer, my friend, was not as informative as Sadia, my companion at the National Gallery. She came to a large round window in stained glass and her eyes lit up. I learnt from her that it was a rose window. And that was it. However, we enjoyed our holiday together, but I decided that those gaps in my education had to be filled.

With Yvonne and I now retired, the first thing we did was to enrol at Birkbeck College, London University, to do a history of art and architecture course. It was a most enjoyable and delightful experience. As part of the course, we visited all the main art galleries in London. These included the National Gallery in Charing Cross, Tate Modern, Tate Britain, the Courtauld Gallery at Somerset House, the British Museum, the Royal Academy of Art, the National Portrait Gallery and the Guildhall Art Gallery in the City of London. The art works we studied were from a wide range of periods and styles, including the Renaissance, Baroque, Rococo, Romantic, Academic, The Pre-Raphaelites, Impressionism, and Modernism.

The lecturer was a Mrs Rosanna Eckersley, and she always opened her lectures with the showing of slides of painters and their paintings, always of a particular style and era. From time to time, all students had to prepare a talk on a particular painter. Essays of 3,000 words had to be written, not only on painters but on buildings of great architectural interest or merit.

Yvonne and I did a really interesting major project on Modernism coming to England. We choose the De La Warr Pavilion in Bexhill-on-Sea as our subject, and we spent a wonderful weekend down there. The managers of the complex went out of their way to assist us, and we got all the information, photographs and tours of the building that were needed for such a project. When we got back to Birkbeck, with the assistance of their visual aids staff, Yvonne and I put a PowerPoint presentation together.

Our talk was a great success.

We visited an art museum roughly every term, studying selected paintings or sculpture in detail. We also completed many more major projects, looking at artistic methods, how both aerial and linear perspective were used or not used, the use of light and shade, symbolism, foreshortening, and realism. Many art exhibitions, featuring some of the world's greatest painters and sculptors, were held from time to time. With our lecturer, we visited most of them.

As was to be expected on such an extensive course, one tends to gravitate towards a particular style, era, or a group of painters. I found myself drifting towards the Impressionists and the Pre-Raphaelites. The former was a progressive group of painters who started the revolution against academic art. The Impressionists went back to nature with the intention of painting only what the eye could see, landscapes directly and freely painted *en plein air* (outdoors). The main Impressionist painters were Cezanne, Degas, Manet, Monet, Morisot, Pissarro, Renoir and Sisley.

The Pre-Raphaelites, also revolutionaries, were a small group of English painters who came together in 1848. Their aim was to challenge conventional views by championing the artists who came before Raphael.

Hunt, Rossetti, Millais, William Morris and Edward Burne-Jones were the leading Pre-Raphaelites. They were supported by John Ruskin, the most prominent art critic of the day.

After seven wonderful years doing this one-day a week course, it finally came to an end. The day came when I received my results by post. On opening the letter, I was overjoyed when I saw that I was awarded the *'Extra Mural Certificate in History of Art and Architecture'* with Merit. A few weeks later I received a lovely postcard of Paul Nash's *Landscape from a Dream* from Mrs Rosanna Eckersley, the lecturer of the class:

> *'Dear Alton,*
>
> *I am so pleased to hear, way back in February, that you now have the Certificate in History of Art and Architecture. Congratulations!*
>
> *I was at a Paul Nash exhibition last week and thought you might like this familiar picture.*
>
> *My summer course is the same as last year, but next year I hope to teach a different one. Maybe see you then. With best wishes to you and Yvonne,*
>
> *Rosanna.'*

As with art and architecture, so too with music.

As mentioned earlier on, I listened to the Tacarigua brass band playing the music of most of the great composers. It has been said that beauty is in the ear, as well as the eye, of the beholder, and the appreciation of a piece of music depends to some extent on the listener's culture and upbringing. It is no wonder then, after spending eight years listening to what we loosely called *classical music* almost every day when I was in the home, that I am an adherent of that genre. There was a drawback though, in that it was all emotional, with no meaningful understanding.

Whilst at Canterbury Christ Church, I met a lawyer friend working and living in the city, who was a great lover of classical music. I accompanied him once to London to see and hear one of the great modern symphony orchestras. These orchestras usually consist of 90 players or more, requiring a large concert hall for their performances. So, it was to the Royal Festival Hall on the South Bank that David and I found ourselves drawn. What an enchanting experience it was for me! The Philharmonic Orchestra played wonderful, wonderful music. A far, far cry from the brass band of Tacarigua orphanage! For me, though, it was still all emotional with no interpretation of the music taking place. I had to do something about this sorry state of affairs. I did this through self-studies at home.

I mentioned previously that rivers and their valleys always have an impact on me. At Tacarigua Orphanage, we spent a lot of time in the river washing, bathing and swimming. In full spate it was an awful sight, a large volume of water rushing downstream at great speed, bulldozing and sweeping away anything in its path: trees, animals, buildings! It was a recurring feature of our lives.

At Boissiere, the other river valley where I lived, the same process occurred every year during the rainy season; extremely heavy rains, followed by a huge volume of brown water roaring downstream, over-flowing its banks and rampaging through the village. It was not until I got to Avery Hill College and took in the Hydraulic Cycle, and actually studying a river from source to mouth, that I got to grips with the dynamics and morphology of rivers. As I mentioned before, their awesome power and destructive force were always a visible feature in my life.

This led me to Smetana's symphonic poem, *Ma Vlast*, which is a musical painting of the River Vltava from its source to its mouth. This composition is played almost every day on Classic FM, a radio station that is only turned off at bedtime in our home. Because of my fixation with river valleys, the tune soon became my favourite, and it is how I progressed from just the emotional phase of listening to music to its interpretation.

The interpretation of Smetana's Ma Vlast

In writing a piece of music, a composer is combining

several important musical elements. Melody, harmony, rhythm, timbre, form, and texture are amongst the primary ones. It is, in fact, the special way in which these musical ingredients are treated, balanced, and combined that brings to any composition its distinctive style or flavour. The music so composed could be programme music, which tells a story, or absolute music which is not trying to describe anything. Smetana's *Ma Vlast* is a symphonic poem, telling a story:

'Two springs pour forth in the shade of the Bohemian forest, one warm and gushing, the other cold and peaceful. Their waves gaily flowing over rocky beds, join and glisten in the rays of the morning sunlight. The forest brooks, hastening on, join and become the River Vltava. Coursing through Bohemia valleys, it grows into a mighty stream. Through thick woods it flows, as the gay sounds of the hunt and the notes of the hunter's horn are heard ever nearer. It flows through grass-grown pastures and lowlands where a wedding feast is being celebrated with song and dance. At the St John Rapids, the stream races ahead, winding through the cataracts, heaving on a path with its foaming waves through the rocky chasm into the broad river channel. Finally flowing on in majestic peace toward Prague and beyond.'

Let us now see how Smetana took the primary ingredients of music listed above, and the musical instruments available to him, to paint a picture, in music, of this river valley.

First, *The Source, Mountain Springs, Dark Bohemian Forest:* The piece begins with the flutes and harps bringing to mind raindrops and the emergence of two rippling springs. The first spring is painted with the strings, the second with the clarinets.

Second, *The Mountain Stream, The Vltava First Emerges:* Strings lead the entire orchestra into musically depicting a powerful mountain spring in a beautiful forest setting.

Third, *The Hunter's Theme:* This is signalled with the horns and trumpets.

Fourth, *Wedding Theme/Polka Celebration*: A wonderful, first pulsating, then dancing, rhythm represents a wedding celebration on the river's banks. The entire orchestra is employed.

Fifth. *Moonlight*: Now on a broader, calmer section of the river valley, Smetana uses muted strings, woodwinds and harps to gently paint this image.

Sixth. *Majestic Vltava:* The Vltava theme is repeated by the whole orchestra.

Seventh. *Rapids:* Turbulent, powerful and unruly.

The Vltava is now a mighty river rushing towards Prague.

Eighth. *Prague and the Mature River:* The Vltava proudly flows through the city and fades into the distance and, eventually, into the North Sea.

A wonderful feature of education is the notion of transfer learning. The man or woman who has acquired knowledge can use it in spheres other than those from whence it came. For instance, the same principles used in the interpretation of Smetana's Vltava are the same ones to be used in a number of compositions, such as:

Vivaldi's *The Four Seasons, which* describes things happening during the year's seasons: such as birds singing in the spring and snowy days.

Beethoven's *Pastoral Symphony,* which describes the peaceful life in the countryside.

Mendelssohn's *Hebrides Overture,* which describes the feel of the sea lapping into Fingal's Cave in the Scottish Hebrides.

Berlioz's *Symphonie Fantastique,* which describes a story he made up himself about a woman he loves. The woman is represented by a tune which is heard in different ways during the symphony; it is the *idée fixe.*

One needs a good ear and an awareness of all

the musical instruments for meaningful understanding. My Tacarigua Orphanage days are a long way behind me now. However, Yvonne and I still spend a lot of our leisure hours listening to many of the wonderful tunes I first heard in Tacarigua. This time, though, it is always a fulfilling experience, as we can interpret, in a delightful way, what we hear.

We now live a life of leisure, but in a sober, moderate, responsible manner. We try to go to any art exhibition held in London, and occasionally we go to see a play. Over the years, we have seen some wonderful plays by some of the greatest playwrights in the world.

A few months ago, we saw an excellent play, *Moon on a Rainbow Shawl* written by Errol John, a Trinidadian and the brother of George, the famous journalist and newspaperman. The play was about a group of Trinidadians living in a barrack yard and their desperate struggles to break out. Because of my experience as a former barrack yard dweller, I found myself deeply involved emotionally, empathising with most of the characters.

I am also a very keen gardener. Every year, the Borough of Thurrock holds a garden competition, 'Thurrock in Bloom'. I enter our back garden as a wildlife garden, and the front as an ornamental one with flowers and shrubs. I am pleased to say in most years I get gold or silver.

The biggest thing in our lives though, since retiring, is going on modest holidays to Europe. By saving a few pounds here and a few pounds there, and choosing our destinations carefully, and always travelling by coach, we invariably find somewhere to go. We have been to most countries in Western Europe but, because of its many varied regions, France is the country we have been to most. However, we are not blasé about anything.

I visited Trinidad in 1997 and went to see Cyril, my brother. He had done very well for himself. Nice home, wife and children. It so happened that Arthur's daughter, Vonneta, was staying for a few weeks. Arthur, our younger brother, had died, and Vonneta was being shunted around all over the place. She was 20. I decided that I might be able to help her. Not help of the instant gratification kind, but long-term, meaningful help. That meant education, or training, or both, and it also meant coming to England. Yvonne and I had everything worked out for her. She came and went up to the University of Nottingham to do her entry exam, but failed it. Sadly, she had to return to Trinidad because she was only here on a student's visa.

After 35 glorious years doing our own thing together, Yvonne and I are in our twilight years. I am 90 and Yvonne is 72. Yvonne is unable to walk or stand up because she has multiple sclerosis (MS), a disease of the nervous system which makes a person unable to control their movements. She is now under the care of some wonderful specialist, trained carers from a company in Thurrock called 'Thurrock Care at Home'.

They come to the home four times a day: morning call about 9 am, lunch-time call at 12.30 pm, tea-time call at 5 pm, and the last call at 6.30 pm. She is totally in their hands because they have to wash and clean her up, dress her and get her in and out of bed via a special hoist. They talk to her all the time, reassuring her that everything is going forward quite smoothly. All the time displaying a great deal of empathy, the ability to understand and share in someone's feelings.

Of course, I am with her all the time except when I go shopping. It will never occur to me to attend any social event and leave Yvonne behind! We follow a special routine, and it works well. All dirty clothes and linen are taken away, washed and brought back on a fortnightly basis. Marks and Spencer do a more than ample range of well-balanced, nutritious microwave meals, so we dine well. We are fortunate to be a 10-minute walk (much less than that if Yvonne is going by special transport) away from Purfleet Care Centre, where our doctors, nurses, dentists and other medical personnel are based.

Yvonne might be handicapped with MS, but she certainly is not vegetating. She is in full possession of all her faculties and spends a great deal of time on her mobile and tablet. We have a comfortable home with prize-winning front and back gardens. I might be 90, but I am no stumbling, dribbling, incoherent old man. I can do most things that a 50-year old can do. Yvonne has her brother, sisters and other relatives who drop in to see us from time to time, but my cousins no longer keep in touch. We have some lovely neighbours who keep an eye on us.

On the whole we are satisfied with our quality of life and are well pleased with what we have accomplished since coming to England some 60 years ago.

Now, the inspiration for this autobiography came from the lecture given by Dr Rowan Williams, as mentioned in my introduction. He posed the rhetorical question, 'What is the purpose of an Anglican university?' and went on to say that he saw all the symbols of a good, functioning Anglican university at Canterbury Christ Church. I feel very uneasy about this, and I am saying this with the utmost humility and respect.

After being in education in England for all these years, both as student and teacher, there are situations that just came to light; the majority of the children that I have taught were not baptised, christened or confirmed, nor were their parents for that matter. Despite the fact that RE is taught in schools, few of them know the true significance of Easter or Xmas; the ten commandments are unknown to them. Not many know about the communion service.

I had an architect student friend from Guyana, Fred, who married an English student from Christ Church and, after qualifying, they both went back to Guyana to settle down. Their first child was on the way when Fred's proud mother donated her christening garments for the christening of her expected grandchild. To her amazement and dismay, her daughter-in-law rejected the offer, saying that she did not believe in such ceremonies. Sadly, the marriage did not last, and the wife returned to England.

I believe that some of the trappings and symbols of Anglicanism are there to be seen at Canterbury Christ Church University. But are they just that? Just mere trappings? It certainly is not the Anglicanism taught by the Church Army when I was a boy at Tacarigua Orphanage. Take the present-day students at Canterbury Christ Church University. Of course, they are all good human beings. They all go about doing their daily chores as is expected of them. They observe the laws of the land and they are all morally sound. If there was a disaster in some obscure part of the world, they would be the first to answer the call for help. They are kind, courteous, and respectful.

However, uppermost in their minds is an education that will guarantee them jobs on graduation. Ironically, most of them behave as though they have a God-given right to the best jobs. If such a job is not forthcoming, they think that their university education was a waste of time! How many of them are baptised and confirmed?

I am suggesting that if Anglicanism is practised at Canterbury Christ Church University, it is very much a watered-down version of the Anglicanism that I was taught by the Church Army at Tacarigua Orphanage all those years ago. However, this should come as no surprise, as we are now living in an open society; questions are asked and no one accepts passively the teachings of the past. Satisfactory answers have to be given, and if they are not forthcoming, then students of today are brave and confident enough to explore other avenues. They may not be practising Anglicans, but they are not uncaring men or women.

Yvonne and I loved Western Europe, and, on retirement, we visited many countries in the region. What made those journeys a little irksome was that one had to produce one's passport as one passed through various countries to get to one's final destination. Almost all our visits were coach tours. Another irritant was that each country had its own currency, so that on arriving home, one had many coins of different denominations which were, more or less, of no use. When England became a member of the Common Market, all those irritants were removed overnight.

I do not pretend to understand what Brexit is all about, but because of the ease of moving from one European country to another, and because I got such pleasure from interpreting the geography and history of the place as we drove through with such ease, it is not to be wondered at that I am a Remainer. As I write, Prime Minister May is furiously fighting to get a deal to satisfy everyone, which is a forlorn hope and she appears to be tearing the Conservative Party apart, if not the whole country.

One thing is certain though, in this country, there is not going to be a bloody revolution, no party or group is going to take up arms. Everything will be settled democratically, but what kind of country will emerge, politically, economically, and even socially, remains to be seen.

Printed in Great Britain
by Amazon

52478862R00059